Stunted Dreams

Stunted Dreams

HOW THE UNITED STATES SHAPED MEXICO'S DESTINY

——

Oscar J. Martínez

El Paso Social Justice Education Project
Printed by CreateSpace, An Amazon.com Company
Available from Amazon.com and CreateSpace.com

First published 2017
by the El Paso Social Justice Education Project
PO Box 12681, El Paso, Texas 79913
http://www.epsocialjustice.org
facebook.com/sjeducationep
info@epsocialjustice.org

Previously published text in Oscar J. Martínez, *Mexico's Uneven Development: The Geographical and Historical Context of Inequality* (New York: Routledge, 2016) is reproduced in this booklet with the permission of Taylor & Francis Publishers. Cover design by Ivelin Buenrostro.

ISBN: 0692909311
ISBN 13: 9780692909317

Introduction

____

Mexico is a predominantly poor country, although a significant portion of its population can be considered middle class and above. Affluence exists side by side with poverty, or, as economists would say, development coexists with underdevelopment. The developed side of Mexico is seen in the prosperous sections of modern urban centers, most notably in major cities like Mexico City, Guadalajara, and Monterrey. But crushing underdevelopment is readily visible in the teeming slums that are usually located on the peripheries of cities, as well as in the thousands of impoverished villages and towns in the countryside. Although current social and economic conditions in Mexico constitute significant improvements over what existed in the nineteenth century and most of the twentieth century, when the country was overwhelmingly poor, in the twenty-first century a majority of the Mexican population still continues to live precariously, with millions mired in extreme poverty. Why is that?

Many people believe that government incompetence, inefficient institutions, and official corruption explain Mexico's troubles. Such maladies of course do harm to any country. Yet, while it is clear that these disorders have been present in Mexico, their dimension and the precise economic damage they have inflicted remain unknown because of the absence of hard data. Such data is difficult to obtain and to measure, and that is the reason no one has come up with scientifically-based findings about this subject. However, the biggest objection to emphasizing ineptitude or wrongdoing in the public sphere to explain Mexico's overwhelming problems is that this approach ignores the "foundational factors" that truly underlie the country's economic quagmire. My recent book, *Mexico's Uneven Development: The Geographical and Historical Context of Inequality*, addresses this subject in detail. The book shows that in order to understand economic outcomes in Mexico over the long term, two situations that are closely intertwined—geographic forces and interaction with the neighboring United States—need to be closely examined.[1] Based on the conclusions reached in *Mexico's Uneven Development*, this booklet explains in a concise manner how Mexico fell into the orbit of the United States and how that reality has greatly affected the fate of the Mexican people.

____

1 Other "foundational factors" examined in *Mexico's Uneven Development: The Geographical and Historical Context of Inequality* (New York: Routledge, 2016) include natural resources, population dynamics, and the structure of production and governance. The reader is referred to that larger work for a comprehensive exposition of the topics treated in this booklet, full citations regarding statistical data and other information, and an extensive bibliography.

The historical record shows that since the beginning of the U.S.-Mexico relationship, the United States has exerted overwhelming influence over the way that Mexico has developed economically. At the most general level, Mexico has benefitted from interaction with its neighbor by channeling most of its (legal and illegal) exports to U.S. markets and by taking in substantial investments by U.S. citizens and corporations. Moreover, millions of impoverished Mexicans have improved their standard of living by resettling in the United States; those same migrants have sent remittances in the billions of dollars to their homeland, providing significant assistance to the Mexican economy. That is the upside of Mexico's strong links to the United States.

What is less known is that the United States long ago undermined Mexico's development prospects by dispossessing Mexico of its most valuable lands, imposing a border that has heavily favored U.S. interests, and paving the way for the powerful U.S. economy to compete more directly with the much weaker Mexican economy. For almost two centuries Mexico has struggled to simultaneously minimize liabilities and maximize benefits as it has navigated its difficult relationship with its wealthy neighbor. The long-felt ambivalence toward the United States is reflected in a statement attributed to President Porfirio Díaz (1876-1880, 1884-1911) and, to this day, frequently repeated by his countrymen: "Poor Mexico, so far from God and so close to the United States."

Before proceeding with our analysis of how the United States has impacted Mexico, let us briefly consider Mexico's situation as a sovereign nation in broad geopolitical perspective.

Fate of Vulnerable Nations Located Next to Imperialistic Countries

---

WORLD HISTORY AMPLY DEMONSTRATES THAT militarily weak countries that possess strategic geographic attributes or valuable natural resources often wind up losing part of their territory and/or come under the political or economic dominance of more powerful neighbors. This is especially true if the terrain of the vulnerable nations is easily penetrable. The legacy of invasion, dismemberment, or subordination leaves victimized countries in a debilitated state from which complete recovery is difficult, if not impossible. Importantly, the potential to become strong and prosperous is seriously undermined for those that lose valuable land or resources. Poland, Ukraine, and Xinjiang provide examples of European and Asian countries that, in centuries past, became targets for conquest, annexation, or control by outsiders bent on fulfilling territorial or geopolitical ambitions. While largely historical, such occurrences have not completely disappeared. In 2014, for example, Ukraine once again lost part of its national territory to a foreign power as Russia invaded and annexed the Crimean peninsula. That act of aggression triggered condemnation of the Russians by the international community.

In the case of Mexico, adjacency to the powerful and hawkish United States led to nineteenth century U.S.-fabricated territorial challenges and disputes, culminating with the devastating loss of half of Mexico's land to its neighbor. At the time Americans subscribed to an expansionist ideology known as "Manifest Destiny," or the belief that the acquisition of new territories would make the United States a great country, fulfilling God's desire for His "chosen" people. The vast open plains of Mexico's northern frontier and the weakly-protected coasts on the Gulf of Mexico and the Pacific Ocean facilitated the invasion of various parts of Mexico by the superior land and sea forces of the U.S. military. At the end of the U.S.-provoked War of 1846-1848, a U.S.-dictated accord, the Treaty of Guadalupe Hidalgo, forced a massive land transfer from Mexico to the United States. That disastrous episode effectively consigned Mexico to a track leading to the underdevelopment of its economy, while, at the same time, the acquired land placed the United States on the road to becoming a world superpower. Gone were the dreams of many Mexicans who, in the years after independence, had foreseen a leading role for their country and a prosperous future for its people; the robust natural endowment contained within the national territory that extended from Alta California in the north to Chiapas in the south framed that optimistic vision. (Figure 1). There is no other comparable instance in world history where land loss by one country and annexation by another has made such a great difference in shaping the destiny of both the conqueror and the vanquished.

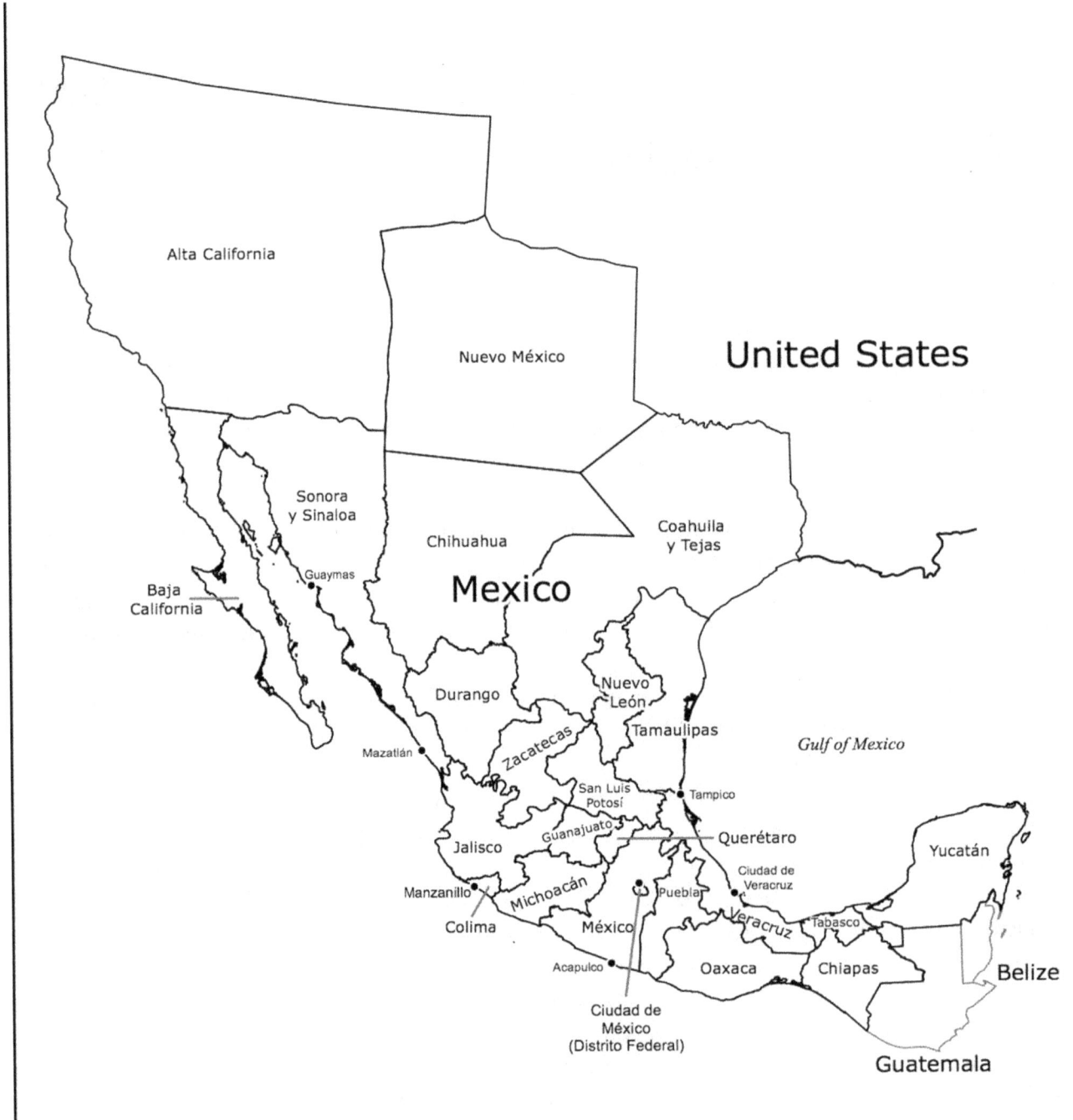

Figure 1. Republic of Mexico, 1824

How Mexico Lost Half its Land to the United States

————

CLASHES BETWEEN MEXICO AND THE United States that eventually led to the great U.S. land grab of the 1840s have their origin in the sixteenth century when European competition for domination of the Americas began. In colonial times, the English, and sometimes also the French, consistently opposed the Spanish presence in the farthest reaches of New Spain (as Mexico was then known), a dynamic that produced conflictive zones from Texas to Louisiana and Florida. Over time, the boundaries of the French and Spanish possessions receded, while the boundaries of the British possessions expanded to the south and the west. The continuous confrontations over control of territory in the border regions created constant friction.

After the United States gained its independence in 1783, it implemented a vigorous expansionist policy that resulted in the acquisition of substantial land from native peoples and territories under the jurisdiction of various nation-states. The limits of the Louisiana Territory became one of the most antagonistic issues in the early nineteenth century as Spain contested U.S. claims far to the west of the Mississippi River. The United States, which had purchased Louisiana in 1803 from France, contended that Texas had been a part of the deal with France, but the Spaniards rejected that claim. Following years of acrimony, the United States and Spain signed a treaty in 1819 that set the borders for Louisiana and recognized Texas as Spanish territory. However, American expansionists continued to stubbornly declare that the United States had "legitimate" rights to Texas. After 1821 newly independent Mexico repeatedly had to resist U.S. efforts to acquire Texas.

In 1836, thousands of Americans and Europeans who had arrived in Texas in earlier years, many without proper documentation, began an uprising against the fledgling Mexican government. The United States capitalized on that rebellion and proceeded to annex Texas in 1845. For Mexico, the annexation of Texas by its neighbor was a major act of aggression, and it led to the deterioration of relations between the two nations. The annexation of Texas directly contributed to the outbreak of war in 1846, a war that turned into a lopsided contest. In the 1840s the United States was already a world power, while Mexico continued to be a severely fragmented society engaged in the initial stages of nation-building. Much better trained and equipped U.S. soldiers invaded Mexico by land and sea.

General Zachary Taylor's troops advanced into Tamaulipas and Nuevo Leon; another army traveled the Santa Fe Trail and penetrated New Mexico, California, and other northern Mexican states; U.S. naval forces joined land soldiers in the invasion of California; finally, in the most important operation of the war, combined U.S. naval and land forces took the port city of Veracruz and then advanced to Mexico City. Control of the capital by the Yankee army gave the U.S. government the upper hand in dictating harsh terms for bringing hostilities to a close in 1848. Years later General Ulysses Grant, who had served as a junior officer with the forces that had invaded Mexico and who occupied the U.S. presidency from 1869 to 1877, characterized the war with Mexico as "wicked" and "the most unjust and most unholy war ever waged by a stronger nation against a weaker one..., an instance of a republic following the bad example of European monarchies, in not considering justice in their desire to acquire additional territory."[2]

Under the terms of the Treaty of Guadalupe Hidalgo, the United States compelled Mexico to accept the 1845 U.S. annexation of Texas and also forced it to cede California, Arizona, New Mexico, Colorado, Nevada, Utah, and parts of Wyoming, Kansas, and Oklahoma. The Rio Grande became half of the new international boundary, with the rest consisting of an irregular line from El Paso del Norte (Ciudad Juárez) to the Pacific Ocean. The United States paid Mexico $18 million dollars for the ceded lands, including $15 million in cash and $3 million in assumed debts that Mexico owed U.S. citizens. In 1853 the United States acquired additional lands from Mexico by buying portions of the states of Sonora and Chihuahua as part of a new pact—variously known as the Gadsden Purchase, Gadsden Treaty, or El Tratado de Mesilla. The $10 million dollar purchase provided the United States with a long-desired land corridor needed to build a railroad along a southern route to California; the Gadsden Treaty also resolved a dispute over the exact location of a small portion of the border that had been set by the 1848 treaty.

As Figure 2 shows, the War of 1846-1848 caused Mexico's territorial domain to shrink by half in comparison to what it had been prior to the Texas insurrection in 1836. The extraordinary value of the territories obtained by the United States dwarfed the compensation received by Mexico. More importantly, the conflict had monumental economic consequences over the long term. It significantly changed the destiny of the United States for the better and radically altered the fate of Mexico for the worse.[3]

---

2 Ulysses S. Grant, *Personal Memoirs of U.S. Grant*, 2 vols. (New York: Charles L. Webster & Co., 1885-1886), vol. 1, p. 53.

3 Excellent maps that show the territorial evolution of Mexico as well as that of the United States are found at https://en.wikipedia.org/wiki/Territorial_evolution_of_Mexico and https://en.wikipedia.org/wiki/Territorial_evolution_of_the_United_States.

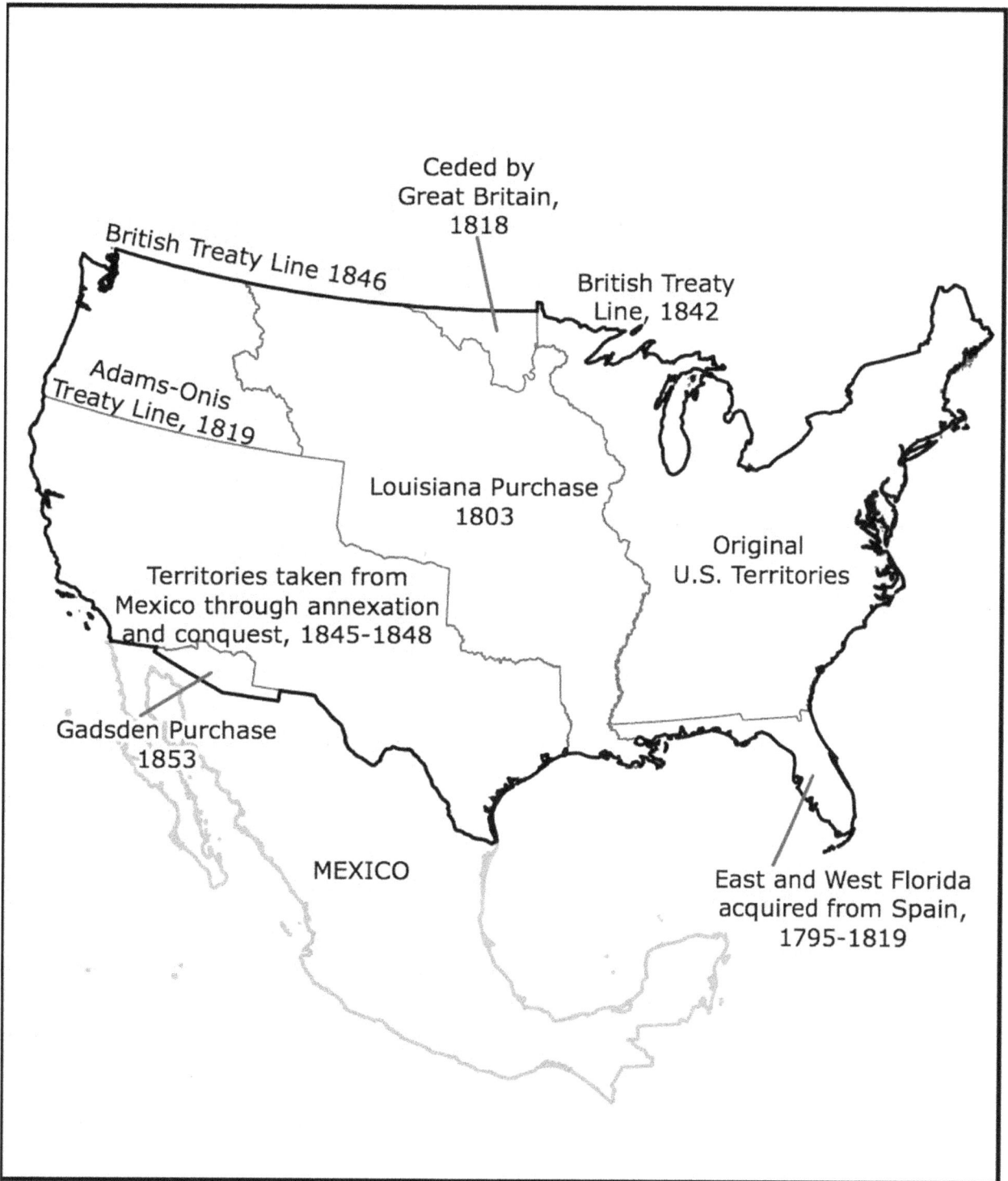

Figure 2. Territorial expansion of the United States and the absorption of Spanish and Mexican territories, 1793-1853

What the United States Gained and Mexico Lost

————

ANNEXATION OF MEXICO'S NORTHERN FRONTIER added 792,000 square miles to the U.S. national domain and along with it a treasure trove of natural riches. President Ulysses S. Grant correctly described the annexed territory as "an empire of incalculable value."[4] Over the last century and a half, the vast resources in the former Mexican lands have contributed enormously to the economic growth and enduring prosperity of the United States. Minerals illustrate that point dramatically: The ceded Mexican territories accounted for 42 percent of the total value of the non-fuel mineral production in the United States in 2008. Seven of the top U.S. non-fuel mineral-producing states had once been part of Mexico's patrimony, including Arizona, which ranked first in the United States with production valued at $7.8 billion dollars; Nevada, second at $6.3 billion; California, third at $4.2 billion; Utah, fourth at $4.1 billion; Texas, sixth at $3.4 billion; and Colorado, ninth at $2.0 billion. For Mexico, the loss of those non-fuel minerals, coupled with the additional loss of fuel minerals, vast fertile lands, fecund forests, and exceptional harbors on the Pacific and Gulf coasts, represent an incalculable economic setback.

The magnitude of Mexico's losses can be gleaned from a cursory assessment of the economic productive capacity of the two most valuable areas in the territories the United States acquired from Mexico—California and Texas. For the United States, these two provinces had stood out as the biggest prizes that needed to be plucked from Mexico.

California was actually considered a larger plum than Texas, and its acquisition brought joy to President James Polk and his fellow expansionists; they had long thought of California as "must have" territory for the United States. U.S. explorers for years had pointed out the great opportunity offered by the world-class harbor at San Francisco bay for conducting trade with Asia. The richly endowed Golden State, as California came to be called, added 163,696 square miles to the national domain. It quickly attracted large numbers of Americans and immigrants from other countries following the discovery of sizable gold deposits in the foothills of the Sierra Nevada in January, 1848, just one month before the signing of the Treaty of Guadalupe Hidalgo. Gold production yielded spectacular wealth for decades, with mines in the Mother Lode gold belt leading the way. In the first five years of the Gold Rush miners extracted about 12 million ounces of

———
4 Grant, *Personal Memoirs of U.S. Grant*, vol. 1, p. 56

gold worth over $16 billion dollars in 2010 prices. With the passage of time gold production in California declined, yet the value of gold output in the state still amounted to $239 million dollars in 2010. Oil is another important commodity that has yielded immense revenues in California for generations, with the state ranking third among the leading oil producing states in the United States in 2014. In addition, because of its ideal climate, robust endowment of fertile land, and abundant water, California early on achieved distinction as a leading agricultural area, rising to become the number one food producer in the United States by the mid-twentieth century; it has retained the top agricultural position to the present. Manufacturing, trade, commerce, tourism and other industries have thrived as well owing to the state's diverse resource base, frontage on the Pacific coast, and splendid ports in San Francisco/Oakland and Los Angeles/Long Beach. In the early years of the twenty-first century California enjoyed high national rankings in various economic categories, including population (1st), state domestic product (1st), manufacturing (1st), market value of agricultural products (1st), crude oil production (3rd), and non-fuel mineral production (6th). If California had been a country in 2015, its economy would have been twice as large as Mexico's entire economy, and the Golden State would have ranked as the 6th largest economy in the world.

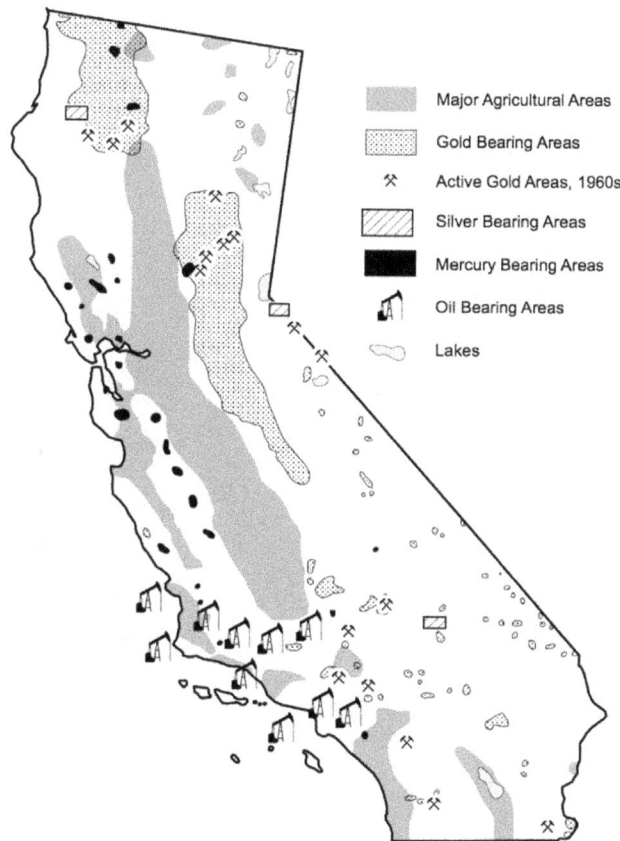

Figure 3. Agricultural and mineral wealth in California, 1970s

The annexation of Texas (with borders as constituted in 1850) by the United States added 268,596 square miles to the national domain. U.S. expansionists coveted Texas because it was rich in natural resources, including a great variety of fertile soils, vast grasslands, nearly 4,000 miles of rivers and other streams, productive coastal areas, a variable climate, dense forests in the eastern part of the state, and a treasure-trove of minerals, most prominently oil and natural gas. The natural endowment of Texas has yielded prodigious wealth over time. In the early 2010s Texas ranked second both in population and in the size of its economy among the U.S. states.

Texans retained the number one ranking in crude oil production, a position they have held for many decades. In 2015 the Texas economy was nearly 30 percent larger than the entire Mexican economy; that year Texas would have ranked 10th in the world if it were a country.

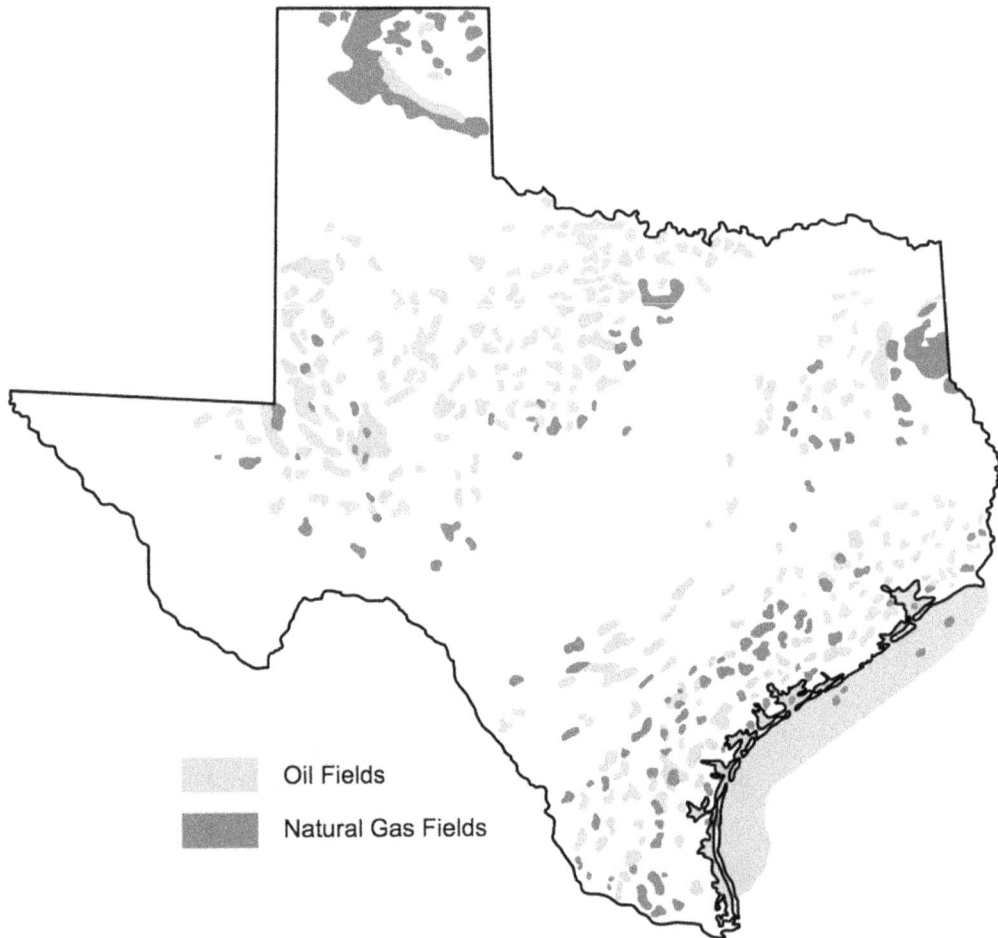

Oil Fields

Natural Gas Fields

Figure 4. Oil and gas fields in Texas, 1960s

Had Mexico retained its northern territories, it unquestionably would have become a much more prosperous country. This is not to say, however, that those areas would have developed in exactly the same way as they have under the United States given all the post-1848 advantages that the ceded lands have had as integral parts of a highly advanced national economy anchored in the mid-western and eastern parts of the United States. But with ownership of California and Texas, for example, Mexico as a nation would have had much more natural assets with which to work to enhance the nation's development capabilities. I have heard it said that retention of the lost lands would not have made much difference for Mexico because Mexican leaders would have followed their "usual misguided policies" and kept the northern frontier underdeveloped. This is a cynical and racist view. The fact is that, historically, those parts of Mexico (such as the Mexico City, Monterrey, and Guadalajara areas) with favorable circumstances have achieved high levels of development.

The Problematic Geography of Mexico's Diminished Territory

───────

IN THE AFTERMATH OF THE mutilation resulting from the war of 1846-1848 and the sale of additional land as part of the Gadsden Treaty, Mexico was left with a much smaller landmass, one that featured a difficult mix of tropical, semitropical, and dry climates and a predominance of mountainous terrain. These conditions meant that only a relatively small portion of the reconfigured Mexican nation would be suitable for habitation or for making a living. Favorable spaces, or areas suitable for population agglomeration and economic productivity, would be few and far between. The troublesome geography would have enormous consequences for the country's development.

MIXED CLIMATE AND SHORTAGE OF GOOD LAND

Scholars have long recognized that many of Mexico's economic problems have their origin in adverse weather conditions, including stifling heat and humidity in tropical areas, scarce moisture in desert zones, and excessive and destructive rainfall in mountain areas. Southeast Mexico, for example, receives up to 120 inches or more of rain annually, while the arid north receives on average only 16 inches. Given that arid lands comprise over half of Mexico's land surface and an additional third are classified as semiarid, the availability of land for cultivation is rather limited. Thus agricultural challenges are considerable. In addition to moisture deficiency in many areas, steep terrain, erosion, bad drainage, and alkali soils conspire to limit Mexico's arable land to an estimated 13 percent of the national territory. To make matters worse, the cultivable land is mostly available in scattered and often isolated tracts. Only a few locations in the country boast large concentrations of good soil placed on well-watered and machine-friendly terrain.

TOPOGRAPHY

The most overpowering physical feature of Mexico is its mountainous terrain, with about 75 percent of the land situated above 3,300 feet above sea level, compared to some 25 percent for the United States and approximately 12 percent for Canada. Western, eastern, and southern Mexico are dominated by the imposing Sierra Madre Ranges, and rugged topography is also found in the Transverse Volcanic Range of central Mexico and the Baja California Peninsular Ranges. The predominance of high altitude living in Mexico is further illustrated by the fact that 80 percent of the population lives above 3,300 feet, compared to less than five percent of the populations of the United States and Canada. Moreover, 20 of the capitals of Mexico's 32 states are situated at over 3,000 feet in altitude, compared to only 7 of the state capitals in the 50 U.S. states. Mexico's contorted landscape became known to the King of Spain in the sixteenth century when the conquistador Hernán Cortés gave his first report on what he had found in the land of the Aztecs. Cortés is said to have crumpled a piece of paper, placed it on a table, and stated simply, "This is Mexico." (See Figure 5).

Figure 5. Topography of Mexico Source: Based on map in James D. Cockcroft, *Mexico's Hope: An Encounter with Politics and History* (New York: Monthly Press, 1998), 8.

Geographers, historians, and other writers have long recognized that the ubiquitous mountains have played a decisive role in the evolution of Mexico. The Sierra Madre Oriental and the Sierra Madre Occidental run parallel to both coasts and practically become one chain in southern Mexico. There the Sierra Madre del Sur rises in Chiapas and continues southward into Guatemala. The western coast is narrow and in some areas the mountains hug the seashore.

Noting the barriers imposed by the Sierra Madre ranges on travel between the interior and the coasts, as well as other problems inherent to Mexico's difficult landscape, prominent U.S. scholar Frank

Tannenbaum concluded in 1950 that "the physical geography could not have been better designed to isolate Mexico from the world and Mexicans from each other." He further observed that travel between Mexico City and Cuernavaca, only 36 air miles apart, required climbing to nearly 10,000 feet and then trekking down a steep descent to 5,000 feet. Tannenbaum added that in many mountain areas of southern Mexico "the pockets that permit towns and villages to survive are often riven and torn, and man holds onto a steep mountainside for a habitat because no other is available."[5]

TRANSPORTATION PROBLEMS

A good transportation infrastructure enhances national economic activity, while a weak infrastructure hinders it. In the case of Mexico, significant challenges have stood in the way of building a strong transportation system. The presence of the formidable mountain ranges paralleling the east and west coasts, coupled with the funnel or triangular shape of the country, limit Mexico mostly to one north-south axis from the northern border to the Isthmus of Tehuantepec. From the Isthmus the axis turns eastward-northeastward, ending on the northern coast of Yucatán. Because of this physical configuration and topography, Mexico lacks the ability of the United States to easily establish and maintain communication and transportation corridors in all directions. A glance at any road or railway map of Mexico will show that the major routes of travel run north-south along the Baja California Peninsula, the West Coast, the Central Plateau, and the East Coast. East-west connections are few and far between simply because of the powerful constraints imposed by the Sierra Madre Oriental and the Sierra Madre Occidental.

The problem with transport in Mexico begins with the almost complete absence of inland navigable waterways that can be used commercially. This is significant because water transportation has always been the cheapest form of hauling commodities, especially heavy freight. In Mexico, only short stretches of a handful of rivers can be navigated, and such rivers are located far from the main centers of population. Today Mexico has approximately 1,800 miles of navigable rivers and coastal canals, which is a small fraction of the 25,000 navigable mileage of the United States. Mexico's great deficiency in this area is a consequence of the unfavorable topography that created short torrential rivers that originate in the highlands and rush quickly to the sea. These rivers have been important for hydroelectric production and for irrigation, but not for transportation. One major problem with respect to navigation is that chronically insufficient rainfall undermines adequate water depths in rivers that otherwise would be more navigable. For example, some rivers that empty into the Gulf, including the Rio Grande and the Pánuco in the North, and the Papaloapan in the South, are navigable from the river mouths into the interior only for short distances because of insufficient water. The Rio Balsas/Lake Chapala/Rio Santiago complex, which flows from the Valley of Mexico to the Pacific Ocean, can be navigated only in parts and has been useful for transport only in a local context. The Rio Lerma, one of the country's most important waterways, was rendered unnavigable by the chronic presence of obstructions like sand and clay, and also because of many manmade structures like dams and low bridges. None of Mexico's waterways even remotely compares

---

5 Frank Tannenbaum, *Mexico: The Struggle for Peace and Bread* (New York: Knopf, 1950), pp. 3-4.

in economic significance to U.S. waterways like the Great Lakes, the St. Lawrence Seaway, the Hudson River/Erie Canal network, the Mississippi River system, and the Intracoastal Waterway.

HIGH COST OF ROADS AND RAILWAYS

Geographical obstacles have made road and railway construction expensive and difficult in Mexico. Prior to the arrival of the railroads in the nineteenth century, people and goods moved along footpaths and dirt roads riddled with so many problems that travel was costly, slow, inconvenient, and even dangerous. Countless roads were little more than well-worn trails that dated back to ancient times. In many places, but especially in the mountains and the jungles, rains or mudslides frequently washed out or blocked roadbeds, posing a chronic challenge to travelers and to those charged with road maintenance. Roadways remained woefully inadequate because chronic lack of resources made regular maintenance practically impossible. Internal political struggles and recurring wars against foreign invaders kept draining the national treasury and handicapped road maintenance efforts. The highways that connected towns in central Mexico with nearby provincial centers and to the seaports received the most attention and were at least kept semi-functional. But the long-distance roads that linked the core region to frontier areas like Yucatán and the Far North evidenced chronic abandonment. The highly deficient transportation in Mexico before the age of the railroads produced disparate domestic economies largely disconnected from one another. Consumption patterns were determined by the foods and raw materials available locally or in nearby surroundings. Many places only 50 or 100 miles away were functionally inaccessible to local people, thus severely restricting both regional and long-distance exchange.

The foreign-financed construction of railways in Mexico in the latter nineteenth century significantly mitigated the transportation problems. But the iron horse would have limited reach among the Mexican population because the tracks largely followed the traditional natural traffic corridors permitted by the country's topography and the routes typically reflected the economic interests of foreign companies rather than broader national needs. Vast areas of Mexico would not be included in the railroad network since they lacked valuable natural resources or population agglomeration. Even so, railroads spawned a major transformation in Mexico by reducing the tyranny of isolation and distance, making the raw materials of the interior lands easier to access, and stringing together a rudimentary national market for the first time. Rail transport also improved Mexico's competitiveness internationally because now it was possible to ship minerals in greater quantities, at cheaper cost, and more rapidly from the mines to the country's ports and beyond. In essence, the railroads created the foundation for the modern Mexican economy.

As with road construction, building the railways in Mexico was a daunting task owing to shortages of capital, the high cost of importing expensive equipment and materials, the high cost of hiring foreign engineers and administrators and, most of all, the need to overcome many hurdles posed by constraining geography. These problems slowed the spread of the railroads in Mexico at a time when the United States rapidly increased its track mileage. For example, by 1910 Mexico had 12,268 miles of railroad track, compared to 250,000 miles in the United States. During much of the twentieth century, the railroads were a major means of passenger travel and freight shipping in Mexico, but eventually decline occurred in both categories. The downturn resulted from neglect when highway construction achieved a higher priority as Mexico embraced motorized transportation. During the age of the North American Free Trade Agreement railroads have made a comeback because of the need for greater freight shipping capabilities.

The improved transportation infrastructure created by the railroads received a major boost with the building of an impressive number of surfaced highways during the twentieth century. Modern roadways could penetrate topographically troublesome areas and reach spaces that the railways could not. As a result, cars, buses, and trucks would eventually haul high volumes of passengers and freight to and from practically every significant urban zone and center of production in the country. Nevertheless, difficult topography constrained the extent and placement of roads and highways, and significant weaknesses can be found in the highway system even today. Mexico's total road and highway mileage adds up to only a small fraction of the total road and highway mileage in the United States, meaning that the density of paved thoroughfares in Mexico is extremely low in comparison to that of the United States; in 2009 about two-thirds of Mexico's long-distance roads (feeder rural and state roads plus free and toll highways) remained unpaved. Although much road upgrading can be done, the Mexican highway network has limited growth potential because of the ubiquitous presence of mountain ranges and because practically all available significant productive areas in the country have already been incorporated into the system. Large areas within Mexico, including thousands of small communities, remain outside the surfaced road system because of their remoteness or lack of economic importance, and chronic shortages of public revenues have meant substandard and erratic road maintenance, which in turn have constantly created interruptions and slowdowns in the flow of traffic. Finally, the expensive tolls charged in recently built modern highways limit the use of such thoroughfares to affluent people, leaving those of modest means to use the older, slower, and more dangerous roadways.

URBAN IMBALANCE

As the history of numerous countries demonstrates, cities have played a gigantic role in generating economic activity and advancing national development. That is because most industrial productivity and innovation takes place in urban spaces. Yet, to achieve high-level economic status, cities need to be situated in favorable surroundings and need to be well connected to the world beyond. Geographic location, the quality of the landscape, and other environmental factors are crucial in determining the level of economic performance of cities. Additionally, ease of transport is especially important. In the case of Mexico, the less than ideal geography in much of the country has constrained transportation and made it expensive, and that situation has contributed significantly to urban imbalance. The elongated, cornucopia-type shape of the country, combined with the high relief in many places, has meant that the distribution of Mexican cities and the distances between them have been greater than would be the case if the country had a rectangular shape and more level terrain—as does the United States. The only—and by far the most important—region of Mexico where inter-urban distances are relatively short is the Central Highlands, meaning the federal district and surrounding states. Cities in the northern border region, in the southern border region, and in the Yucatán peninsula are located far from the heartland. It has been only since the recent completion of surfaced highways to these far-flung areas that substantive incorporation of the distant cities into the national economy began to take place. By contrast, in the United States the West is the only region where substantial distances separate cities. In the eastern third of the United States— historically the most populated and most economically dynamic region of the country—the distances are much shorter because of prevailing flat terrain and because the population centers are more concentrated and clustered close to one another.

Another important issue for Mexico is that its urban population has been overwhelmingly concentrated in the interior of the country at a significant distance from the ocean, resulting in relative isolation from the rest of the world. By contrast, both the urban and rural population of the United States has been overwhelmingly located along the Atlantic, Gulf, and Pacific shorelines, and adjacent to the Great Lakes and the major inland rivers. These U.S. areas are prime locations for trade and lend themselves naturally to economic specialization. To be sure, Mexico has coastal cities, but, apart from serving as commercial ports of modest importance and tourist resorts, Mexico's seaside towns historically have been of secondary significance in the national urban configuration. Mexico has been, and continues to be, an inland nation, with its largest and most important urban centers situated in the interior plateaus, plains, basins, and valleys, distant from and totally lacking in direct connection to the ocean via inland waterways. In the United States in 2016, seven of the ten largest metropolitan areas were situated by the ocean, in contrast to only one for Mexico—Tijuana, Baja California, which fronts on the Pacific Ocean. But, significantly, Tijuana is not even a seaport as a consequence of its lack of a natural harbor and its close proximity to San Diego, California, a U.S. urban center that is endowed with a superb bay. The reality is that Mexico does not have a bona-fide seaport metropolis on the scale of even small U.S. ports like Jacksonville, Florida, much less world-class mega ports like Shanghai or Hong Kong.

A final observation regarding Mexico's urban landscape is that many cities are located at high altitudes, while few U.S. cities are so situated. For example, 20 of Mexico's 32 state capitals/federal entities have altitudes over 3,000 feet, compared to only 6 of the 50 U.S. state capitals. Just one of the U.S. state capitals is over 7,000 feet (Santa Fe, New Mexico, at 7,200 feet), while the following Mexican state capitals/federal entities surpass 7,000 feet: Toluca (8,793 feet), Zacatecas (8,189 feet), Pachuca (7,959 feet), Mexico City (7,546 feet), Tlaxcala (7,388 feet), and Puebla (7,093 feet). The presence of many high-altitude cities in Mexico has significant economic implications, including greater expense in building and maintaining transportation links with the rest of the country. Cities located in the plains, as is typically the case in the United States, have the great advantage of being more easily connected to each other and to the nation as a whole because highways are more direct and travel times are shorter. The United States, England, Germany, and France are examples of countries where, because of favorable geography, transportation development has been relatively easy, cities have flourished, and the economy has prospered.

In his 1938 landmark article on geopolitics, Nicholas J. Spykman concluded that Mexico's physical space, its internal environmental conditions, and its juxtaposition with the powerful United States would severely limit Mexico's future economic prospects. Spykman wrote: "The shape of the North American continent prevents Mexico from adding significantly to its size by southern expansion, and topography and climate will make it *forever impossible* [emphasis mine] to build on its area a powerful economy."[6] Up to the present, Spykman's observation has been on target. Mexico has been historically unable to build a powerful economy along the lines of the United States or the advanced countries of Europe and East Asia; rather, Mexico's economy remains half-developed and half-underdeveloped. Moreover, before the 1980s growth and productivity were largely anchored on oil and other raw materials, and since then they have rested on the low-cost human labor that drives today's foreign-dominated, export-oriented industrial sector. Mexico's present large economy may be considered "powerful" by some because of the nation's lofty GDP (Gross Domestic Product) ranking, but in truth Mexico is mostly a low-wage assembly country at the service of multi-national corporations. Geography has much to do with that reality.

---

6 Nicholas J. Spykman, "Geography and Foreign Policy, Part II," *The American Political Science Review* 32:2 (April, 1938), p. 226.

U.S. Leverage over Mexico's Economy

——

THE BORDER IMPOSED BY THE United States in the mid-nineteenth century allowed the powerful U.S. economy to draw much closer to Mexico's main population centers and consumer markets, with the result that, in a rather short amount of time, Americans established economic dominion over their neighbor to the south. The proximity of U.S. industry and commerce had the effect of undermining the development of domestic industrial and commercial sectors in Mexico. Having less productive capacity, Mexican manufacturers, merchants, and entrepreneurs found it very difficult to compete with their stronger U.S. counterparts. U.S. manufacturers produced better and cheaper products because they had more capital and could afford the latest technologies, especially in mass assembly operations. Concurrently, U.S. merchants had the advantage conducting business because they had bigger enterprises and better connections and outlets than Mexican merchants. Consequently, from the beginning of Mexico's independence, consumer products from the United States (and also from England, France, and Spain) flooded Mexican markets—both legally and illegally. U.S. corporations would capitalize on Mexico's weak economic situation by enticing Mexican elites into accepting partnerships and joint ventures. Such alliances would prove lucrative for those involved, but not for Mexico's home-grown industries. The end result would be pronounced Mexican economic dependence on foreign countries, most notably the United States.

TRADE

As a long-time developing country, Mexico's exports to other countries have consisted predominantly of agricultural products, precious metals, industrial minerals, and light manufactures, while imports have consisted largely of capital goods such as equipment, machinery, tools, and vehicles, in addition to high- and low-end consumer goods produced by advanced technologies in developed countries. Mexico's trading posture has put the country at a great disadvantage because the combination of exporting basic products and importing finished goods does not foster genuine economic development. This is especially true because the United States, the most powerful economy in the world, has long been Mexico's chief trade partner. At present approximately three quarters of Mexico's exports go to the United States and half of Mexico's imports come from the United States. Those percentages underscore the fact that the United States dominates Mexico's trade, a reality that goes back to the nineteenth century. For generations Mexico tried to shield its domestic industries from U.S. and other foreign competition by enacting protectionist measures on legally-traded goods and making efforts to control the influx of contraband. Those initiatives, however, yielded limited results.

Tariffs and other trade barriers imposed by the Mexican government in the generations prior to the enactment of NAFTA (North American Free Trade Agreement) never worked well because of the ease with which foreigners could circumvent them and because Mexico lacked the capacity to stop smuggling on its porous 2000-mile northern border and its unprotected coasts. Let's look at some historical examples. After independence, Mexico imposed ad valorem tariffs on imports both to raise revenues for government operations and to protect domestic industries. Normally tariffs supplied between a third and a half of the government's revenues. The first tariff law in Mexico set an ad valorem tax of 25 percent on all imports and prohibited the importation of nine foreign products. The tariff increased sharply after 1823 and the number of prohibited imports rose as well. On the list of prohibited goods were products that competed with domestic goods, such as metals, textiles, cotton and woolen cloth, timber, and a variety of foodstuffs. By the 1840s the ad valorem rate reached 45 percent and the number of prohibitions rose to about 60 items.

Despite the protective barriers, a high volume of allowable foreign goods entered Mexico without paying the required duties, as did multitudes of prohibited foreign products. Government officials, intellectuals, industrialists, and businesspeople expressed alarm at the harm that contraband inflicted on the state in the form of unpaid customs duties and the damage done to vulnerable domestic industries that could not compete with cheap imports. In 1823 Mexico's Minister of Finance referred to contraband as "scandalous," "disastrous," and "punitive," and called smugglers "villains" and "traitors." Well-placed sources calculated that Mexico lost up to 75 percent of all tariff revenues due to smuggling. Henry G. Ward, the British charge d'affaires, expressed his belief that contraband was "infinitely greater" than legal commerce. The U.S. minister to Mexico, Joel R. Poinsett, not only recognized the prevalence of the illicit trade but admitted significant complicity among Americans. "I regret to state that the organized system of smuggling, carried on by American vessels…justifies the officers of this [Mexico's] government in regarding with suspicion every vessel sailing under our flag," Poinsett wrote to U.S. Secretary of State Henry Clay in 1826.[7] Perhaps two thirds of all imports from the United States between 1821 and 1845 entered Mexico illegally.

The difficulty of controlling contraband intensified during and after the U.S.-Mexico War of 1846-1848. The free-flowing trade imposed by the U.S. occupation forces became institutionalized as U.S. and Mexican merchants capitalized on lucrative opportunities and Mexican consumers became accustomed to acquiring foreign products at reduced prices. Smuggling increased between 1858 and 1905 when select northern Mexican states declared their border communities as free trade zones and later when the federal government converted the entire border area into a Zona Libre, or free trade area. Frontier towns were

---

7 Poinsett quote from Walther L. Bernecker, "Contrabando: Ilegalidad y corrupción en el México decimonónico," *Espacio, Tiempo y Forma*, Serie V, H. Contemporánea, 6 (1993), pp. 396, 402.

granted import privileges to better deal with their precarious economic situation in the face of crushing competition from powerful U.S. manufacturers and merchants directly across the border. During the time that the Zona Libre functioned, *fronterizos* (Mexican borderlanders) could import foreign goods without having to pay the usual tariffs. Under such circumstances, commerce and other economic activities improved in the Mexican border region, lessening the need for struggling fronterizos to move elsewhere, as many had done before the arrival of the Zona Libre. At the same time, however, untaxed foreign imports made their way illegally from the Zona Libre to the interior of Mexico, where they inflicted harm on domestic manufacturers and merchants.

Contraband from the United States to Mexico thrived for generations until the commencement of the age of trade liberalization in Mexico in the 1980s, when tariffs began to fall. In 1994 NAFTA ushered in the eventual elimination of import taxes on many products, bringing about a fundamental change in the nature of border contraband. Smuggling became less organized. During the pre-NAFTA days, many shady business concerns and contraband rings from Brownsville-Matamoros to San Diego-Tijuana had supplied Mexicans with a great variety of smuggled goods at prices well below those of legally-imported merchandise. Trucks loaded with bootleg products like weapons, ranges, refrigerators, freezers, washing machines, television sets, typewriters, video cassette recorders, electronic gadgets, computers, clothes, foodstuffs, automobiles, etc. made regular runs from the border to cities like Monterrey, Saltillo, Torreon, Chihuahua, Hermosillo, Guadalajara, Mexico City, and many others. Repeating an old familiar story that dated back to the early nineteenth century, Mexican business and industrial leaders complained time and again regarding the harm that smuggling did to their interests, insisting that the federal government had to do more to address the problem. And Mexico City responded as it had in previous generations, periodically cracking down on the contraband trade by firing corrupt customs agents, tightening up regulations, increasing vigilance in the nation's ports of entry, and enacting "buy Mexican" campaigns.

Although NAFTA has greatly reduced the smuggling of consumer merchandise into Mexico, the problem has not been eliminated completely. Foreign products not covered by the agreement have continued to make their way across the border illegally, thus continuing to undermine Mexico's domestic industries. The greatest damage to Mexican manufacturers and farmers, however, has actually come from the now-permitted legal entry of foreign consumer goods that were formerly banned or taxed at high levels. Such products have flooded the country, leading to deindustrialization in the cities and massive job losses in agriculture in the countryside. In short, NAFTA has significantly increased Mexico's dependence on the United States.

FOREIGN INVESTMENT

Mexico's traditional need to seek money from foreigners is rooted in the country's limited capacity to generate sufficient internal capital to fuel the economy and provide revenues for government operations. Problematic geography has been a major contributor in this respect. For example, before the onset of the railroad age, difficult topography spawned a highly inefficient land transportation system that undermined the exploitation of mineral resources, the country's major natural asset. Since Mexico lacked navigable inland waterways, land travel was the only option to move bulk commodities within the country and to the major coastal ports. Yet travel on primitive, ill-kept, and generally dreadful roadways was not only difficult but exceedingly costly because of the ubiquitous mountainous terrain. Agricultural land, Mexico's other natural asset, also offered limited possibilities for capital formation not only because of the transportation problem, but more fundamentally because the overall endowment of fertile soil was small in size and the best farming areas were confined to the Central Highlands and otherwise scattered locales around the country, rather than being concentrated in contiguous sizable tracts such as was the case in the rich agricultural regions of the Midwestern United States. While modernization has improved Mexico's capital-generating capacity, the country still lags far behind the advanced economies of North America, Europe, and East Asia, and must therefore continue to seek investments from abroad.

Americans and Europeans began channeling capital to Mexico early in the nineteenth century, but they were particularly active at the turn of the twentieth century, during the time of the Porfirio Díaz dictatorship. By 1910 foreigners owned over a third of the land in Mexico, with Americans holding some 130 million acres. Mexico's mines and oil fields also fell into foreign hands, with external capital constituting 98 percent of the capital invested in the largest mining companies and 100 percent among the largest oil companies. Infrastructure industries such as railways and public services such as electricity and telephones were also largely owned by foreigners. Things changed as a result of the Mexican Revolution (1910-1920), when Mexico started a campaign that eventually resulted in the nationalization of much of the land and other interests held by foreigners, significantly reducing the degree of external control over the Mexican economy. During the post-World War II period, however, a new wave of foreign capital made its way into Mexico. By 1964 U.S. capital totaled $1.3 billion dollars, by far the largest sum among investors from other countries. Once again, large portions of the Mexican economy fell into the hands of multinational corporations. Foreign firms controlled or had significant influence over 58 percent of the largest 400 companies operating in Mexico either through full ownership or through affiliation with Mexican investors.

In 1965 U.S. corporations involved in manufacturing began setting up assembly operations in Mexico's northern border cities under the newly created Border Industrialization Program. The Mexican government enticed foreign companies to relocate with guarantees of 100-percent ownership of their firms and duty-free importation of machinery and inputs used in the assembly plants, which became known as *maquiladoras*. Mexico's northern frontier proved highly attractive for multinationals because the border economy was closely linked with that of the United States and because cheap local labor was readily available. A decade later maquiladoras began appearing in select areas of Mexico's interior. With the enactment of NAFTA in 1994, the foreign-controlled assembly manufacturing sector in Mexico experienced explosive growth, emerging as the most important industrial activity in the country. In 2001, nearly 4,000 maquiladoras employed approximately 1.3 million workers.

NAFTA stimulated a sharp increase in new FDI (foreign direct investment) in Mexico as the Mexican government agreed to extend new protections to private property, including guarantees against expropriation. Incoming FDI skyrocketed beyond $20 billion annually after 2000, with U.S. capital composing about 70 percent of the total. Since export-oriented production drew most of the FDI, Mexico's exports recorded spectacular growth in a short period of time, tripling in value between 1994 and 2002. Manufactures became the predominant exports by far, reaching nearly 85 percent of Mexico's exports by 2010. Advocates of free markets heaped praise on Mexico for reinventing itself into one of the most open economies in the world and becoming a haven for external capital. They cited the remarkable growth in manufacturing exports as evidence of the success of the open-borders, free-markets strategy.

Yet, while overall numbers are impressive, the increases in FDI and manufactured exports have not translated into the life-improving development that most Mexicans hoped for when the country adopted the open-trade economic model. Products assembled in maquiladoras, whose components with rare exception originate with home companies in the United States or are made in U.S. subsidiaries located on Mexican soil, make up over half of Mexico industrial exports. Such exports clearly are not bona-fide Mexican products. FDI has also done little to create jobs that are firmly rooted in Mexico's domestic economy or that pay high wages. Over three-quarters of the employees in the maquiladora industry are ordinary, low-paid workers.

Today the Mexican economy is dominated by foreigners, just as it was during the time of Porfirio Díaz over a century ago. The automobile industry is perhaps the largest externally-controlled industry, with General Motors, Ford, Chrysler, Nissan, Volkswagen, Honda, and Toyota ranking as the major car producers. In the finance sector, foreigners own three-quarters of all assets held by Mexico's banks. Even retailing has fallen largely into U.S. hands. That is exemplified by the incredibly rapid expansion of Wal-Mart since the 1990s. Wal-Mart, which through buy-outs of Mexican firms grew to become Mexico's largest retailer as well as the top private-sector employer, operated more than 2,400 retail outlets in Mexico in 2017, including Superstores, Sam's Clubs, Superamas, Suburbias, Bodega Aurreras, and sundry other department stores and restaurants.

Border Issues and U.S. Policies

———

When Donald Trump launched his campaign for the 2016 U.S. presidential election, he accused Mexico of sending its worst people to the United States, namely "criminals," "drug traffickers," and "rapists," and, he "assumed," some "good people" as well. That statement, plus many other slanderous attacks that Trump hurled at Mexicans during the course of the campaign, won him strong support among many American voters who harbored anti-Mexico and anti-immigrant sentiments. Without the backing of that sector of the electorate, who also embraced Trump's advocacy of a "border wall" and a ban on Muslim immigration, it is unlikely that Trump would have won the election. Trump's tirade against Mexico illustrates the deep-seated animosity toward Mexicans that has traditionally existed in the United States, an enmity rooted in racism but also influenced by cross-border undocumented migration and drug trafficking.

Certainly long before Trump ran for president U.S. politicians and the American public in general constantly blamed Mexico for not doing enough to lessen the need for so many poor Mexicans to migrate abroad and for failing to crack down on criminal organizations involved in the drug trade. Over the last century the U.S. government has passed punitive laws, enacted harsh policies, and increasingly militarized the U.S.-Mexico border. Conversely, Mexicans blamed the United States for creating the demand for both cheap labor and illicit drugs, unleashing forces in Mexico to supply those needs. The historical record shows that the two problems are deeply embedded on both sides of the border. It is a fact that Mexico's economy has been unable to provide sufficient good-job opportunities for its people, compelling many poor Mexicans to take the international migration route or to join the drug trade. But, it is also a fact that for generations there has been an insatiable demand in the United States for Mexican cheap labor and illicit narcotics.

So, where do these two problems originate? On the demand side or the supply side? Simple economics teach us that demand begets supply, so logically the origin rests with the United States. The U.S. economy and American consumers are the drivers of both undocumented migration and drugs, and Mexicans play the role of accommodating partners by providing cheap labor and illicit narcotics. It is worth asking—what if the demand for migrants and drugs north of the Rio Grande did not exist? A reasonable answer is that these issues would be inconsequential in the U.S.-Mexico relationship.

Responsibility aside, the reality is that the impact of undocumented migration and drug trafficking has been deeply felt on both sides of the border in both positive and negative ways. In the United States, the presence of unauthorized immigrants has brought many economic benefits, but such an advantage has been tempered by tensions in American society over presumed job competition and the alleged high cost of providing tax-supported services to immigrants. With respect to drug trafficking, the availability of illicit narcotics has had many undesirable consequences, including social problems linked to addiction and violence in major cities like Chicago. Further, combatting the drug war has required high public expenditures.

How has Mexico been affected by the massive exodus of its people to the United States? Outmigration has long served as a safety valve, sparing Mexico of social pressures and tensions that would otherwise arise if migrants stayed home. Furthermore, over the generations Mexicans working abroad have sent large amounts of money to their homeland in the form of remittances, and this has greatly helped millions of families and boosted the Mexican economy. On the negative side, those same families have become dependent on the remittances, a risky situation indeed given the challenges that breadwinners have confronted crossing the U.S.-Mexico border and the uncertainties they have faced finding and holding jobs in a U.S. economy subject to recurring recessions. Moreover, the separation of families for prolonged periods has created serious social problems and led to delinquency among young people who have grown up in households with absentee parents. The exodus of so many workers from Mexico has also spawned labor shortages in agriculture and other sectors of the Mexican economy. Moreover, Mexican workers have been subjected to exploitation, discrimination, and physical abuse in the United States. Since the election of President Trump, undocumented immigrants have lived in great fear as deportations have risen to new levels, tearing apart many families in the process. Worst of all, over the last three decades, thousands of undocumented migrants have died from exposure attempting to cross dangerous stretches of the U.S.-Mexico borderlands, to include the Rio Grande region, the Arizona desert, and arid and mountainous sections of Southern California.

With respect to the drug trade, Mexico has benefitted economically from the influx of billions of "dirty" U.S. dollars. However, the lawlessness attendant to drug trafficking has seriously undermined the authority of the state, compromised institutions, bolstered corruption, destroyed the rule of law, required large expenditures for military and law enforcement operations, and produced catastrophic levels of violence, especially in border communities. Shockingly, between 2007 and 2016, over 200,000 homicides occurred in Mexico, far surpassing the number of homicides in war-torn countries like Afghanistan and Iraq. Drug trafficking has transformed border cities like Tijuana, Ciudad Juárez, and others into battlegrounds as criminal organizations have ferociously fought each other as well as law enforcement for the privilege of conducting their nefarious activities without obstruction. In short, the drug trade has devastated many parts of Mexico and made life increasingly dangerous for its citizens. That is a high price to pay for satisfying the demand for illicit narcotics in the United States.

In considering the underlying conditions that have fostered outmigration and stimulated the drug trade in Mexico, we need to reference the role of geography once again. Both problems are clearly linked to insufficient economic opportunity in the physical space that the Mexican people occupy. The scarcity of good jobs is inherently tied to Mexico's difficult landscape and less than ideal climate—largely mountainous and excessively arid. And, ultimately, Mexico's problematic geography is an outcome of history, specifically the loss of extremely valuable territories to the neighboring United States. The other geographic problem linked to that history is that the border that the United States imposed allowed the powerful U.S. economy to draw closer to Mexico's heartland, thus bringing crushing and enduring competition to Mexican industrial and commercial interests. The end result is that, lacking a strong economic foundation, Mexico has been unable to provide enough decent jobs for the impoverished half of its population. In desperation, many Mexicans have opted to migrate abroad or join the drug trade. One might wonder to what extent undocumented migration and drug trafficking might exist today if Mexico had been able to hold on to its northern territories in the nineteenth century. If economic giants like California and Texas were still a part of Mexico, the country's foundational factors would be much stronger. These areas would provide the opportunities that do not exist south of the Rio Grande, and Mexicans would have much less need to leave their homeland or enter the world of criminality in pursuit of a better life. Most importantly, a much more equal relationship would exist between Mexico and the United States.

Conclusion

————

By highlighting unfavorable conditions related to Mexico's interaction with the United States, it has not been my intent to exonerate Mexicans from any blame for the country's lackluster economic performance. There is no denying that much of the criticism directed at the Mexican government regarding issues like corruption, erratic policy-making, or malfunctioning institutions is justified. But the aim of this booklet has been to point out that Mexico's underdevelopment cannot be explained simply by focusing on easily noticeable maladies that are common to many countries, including the United States. Underlying, or deeper causations, are far more important for understanding the difficult context that Mexico has had to confront, and these fundamental causations demand our attention above and beyond "low-hanging fruit." The rocky relationship with the United States and the problems spawned by a troublesome geography constitute paramount foundational factors in the case of Mexico, and they go a long way toward explaining the country's unsatisfactory economic progress.

Without question the loss of Mexico's most valuable lands to the United States as a consequence of the U.S.-Mexico War of 1846-1848 and the subsequent dominance of the powerful U.S. economy over the Mexican economy have played major roles in shaping the destiny of the Mexican people. The momentous events of the nineteenth century evaporated Mexico's dreams of national greatness and widespread domestic prosperity. By contrast, the valuable territories annexed from Mexico and the relocation of the border farther to the south helped the United States substantially in its quest to become an economic and military superpower.

Significantly, Mexico is the only developing country in the world situated next to the most advanced country on the planet, and that is a prime reason why the Mexican economy has not flourished in the same manner as those of other recently-industrialized countries such as China, South Korea, or India. A key major difference is that these nations have not had to contend with a colossus as their next-door neighbor. Mexicans have had to struggle much harder to build their economy under the mammoth shadow of the United States, not unlike small retailers who try to survive in the face of crushing competition from a Wal-Mart megastore located uncomfortably nearby.

But what about Canada? It too is contiguous with the United States, yet Canada managed to become a developed country. What makes Canada different from Mexico? Importantly, Canada has evolved in a much more advantageous international and environmental context than Mexico, to include having escaped invasion by the United States, not losing any of its lands to its expansionist neighbor, having its relatively small population (36 million people compared to 127 million for Mexico) concentrated along one of the best endowed swaths of land in North America, and possessing robust natural resources to complement its industrial economy. And yet, like Mexico, Canada has also experienced the smothering of its domestic industries as a consequence of the daunting presence of U.S.-controlled subsidiaries, or branch plants. Canadian scholars and other analysts have produced a voluminous literature documenting the high degree of external dependence of Canada's manufacturing sector, the concentration of Canadian trade with the United States, the relatively low level of research and development carried out in Canada, and the "invasion" of U.S. brands ranging from automobiles to home appliances and fast-food chains. Mexicans and Canadians, it turns out, do share some commonalities in their relationship with the United States. But, what makes Mexico different is that, as an economically and politically frail country, its bargaining position vis-à-vis the United States has been far weaker than that of Canada's.

If Porfirio Díaz were still around, he would be amazed at the continuing relevance of his observation of long ago, "Poor Mexico, so far from God and so close to the United States."

www.ingramcontent.com/pod-product-compliance
Lightning Source LLC
Chambersburg PA
CBHW081012040426
42443CB00016B/3495